Other books by A. E. Fonner (Al Fonner):
Ones Such as These [ISBN 0-595-22346-X]

Reborn

and Other Versifications

A. E. FONNER

iUniverse®

REBORN AND OTHER VERSIFICATIONS

iUniverse books may be ordered through booksellers or by contacting:

iUniverse
1663 Liberty Drive
Bloomington, IN 47403
www.iuniverse.com
1-800-Authors (1-800-288-4677)

Because of the dynamic nature of the Internet, any web addresses or links contained in this book may have changed since publication and may no longer be valid. The views expressed in this work are solely those of the author and do not necessarily reflect the views of the publisher, and the publisher hereby disclaims any responsibility for them.

Any people depicted in stock imagery provided by Thinkstock are models, and such images are being used for illustrative purposes only. Certain stock imagery © Thinkstock.

ISBN: 978-1-5320-3558-6 (sc)
ISBN: 978-1-5320-3559-3 (e)

Library of Congress Control Number: 2017918518

Print information available on the last page.

iUniverse rev. date: 12/07/2017

This collection of poems is dedicated to all those who walk the Earth—happy or sad, lonely or comforted, depressed or exhilarated, angry or joyous. We are all cut from the same cloth and belong to that same enigmatic club that is humanity.

Contents

Preface

To a growing boy, poetry consists of nursery rhymes, children's songs, and crude verses told around the playground. In middle school and high school, I became acquainted with Lord Byron, William Wordsworth, and Emily Dickinson. My eleventh-grade English teacher even went so far as to teach us about meter and forced us to memorize several of the classics. I thought Edgar Allan Poe had some poems worthy of my consideration, maybe because they had a certain eclectic quality. I also saw value in Shakespeare's work, where his lines flowed like rivers through all manner of landscapes and climates.

I am quite sure that I always wanted to write. I can remember playing on my mom's clunky old black typewriter. It was not electric; one had to bang away at the keys furiously to cause the type to strike the paper, while the black ribbon edged cautiously forward from one spool to the next. Of course, it was all gibberish, but it was great fun. I always pictured myself as a journalist, breaking some big story that exposed corrupt politicians or crime bosses. Perhaps a great novel or short story would pour forth onto the pages as I tapped away on the typewriter keys or scribbled heatedly with my sharpened number-two lead pencil on a pad of paper. Later in life, I did manage to publish one novel, which is another story—but serious poetry?

The thing about poetry is that it is very personal. I think a poet is suddenly inspired and locks him- or herself off in some closet to breathe life with words into the idea that had struck. When poets are done, what have they to show for their effort? A few lines on paper that may or may not rhyme. Those lines may have some semblance of rhythm or meter, or perhaps they do not. The poet's work may be embraced by an audience, or it may be destined to banishment in a drawer or box. One thing is for sure, though: the poet will feel a sense of personal accomplishment and pride, having finished. That is why writing poetry is so personal.

How someone judges a poem's worth can be based on many things. A poem written by an acknowledged great poet, past or present, is worth a great deal more than one written by an unknown novice. Poetic works penned by celebrities certainly flame the hearts and minds of their audience, ballooning the value of the work to astronomical proportions. The poem's subject can make it worthier of acclaim to certain readers. The writer's use of language and style can impact the poem's appeal to the reader. I am reminded of the movie *Dead Poets Society*, where Robin Williams's character, John Keating, is mocking a textbook author's method of scoring a poem using a sliding scale that considers such attributes as length of the poem and its meter. I think that a poem's value to the reader is based on his or her own experiences, hopes, dreams, and desires.

The process of writing a poem has largely been one of inspiration. Something strikes me; it could be an idea, an emotion, an encounter, a person, or an event. Whatever stimulates me, my mind becomes haunted, so to speak, and the lines begin to form. I put them down on whatever is available. The best poems I've written, I believe, are the ones where I do not think too hard about it. The words flow, and I have a completed draft in about a half hour for shorter poems. Longer ones may take a day or two. When I try too hard and force the words, the poem does not work; it was not meant to be.

Writing poetry, for me, has at least two purposes. First, writing poetry satisfies, at least in part, my creative need.

Second, it has a therapeutic element. Let me address these further.

The creative process allows me to reflect on my inner self at that moment when the poem is conceived, giving it life in an expressive way. I believe creativity is one way that God manifests his presence in our lives. The Bible says that God created the heavens and the Earth and everything that swims in the waters and moves on the land. He then created man in his own image. God is creative, so it makes sense that we, his creation, are creative. Creativity compels us to produce something that is an extension of ourselves. This creativity allows us to touch others in a profound way.

The second purpose, therapeutic, is more personal. We are social creatures who desire a connection with others and, just as importantly, our origin.[1] When I say "origin," I am referring to whatever story of creation the reader accepts as his or her own. isolation from others, separation from our origin, or both, causes turmoil within, leading to stress, anger, and depression. Writing poetry allows me to discipline the thoughts and emotions that sway me one way or the other. Through sharing my poems with others, I achieve a connection with the audience and become part of their community. Poetry also provides me a way to God's ear. This makes sense because, when I think about the songs of the Native Americans, the chants sung in a drafty monastery, and even the psalms of the Bible, all are a form of poetry. Imagine how David poured out his heart to God with each line of a psalm as he composed it, or consider the prayers lifted to their deities as the Plains Indians sang their songs in the twilight of a summer's night. Poetry expresses our bonds as community and our relationship with our origin.

The poems in this collection I have written over the past few years. They are arranged in a fashion that demonstrates my personal growth and are collected works that illustrate the progression I think we all go through as we make sense of the world around us and our lives in it. So, we begin with "Lost in the Darkness," the poems that were expressions of me at some of my lowest points. These poems display the pain, fear, anger, hopelessness, and doubt I felt at various times. They were my cry to God from the darkness. These are followed by "Through the Twilight." This section includes poems that were written during those times when I could sense the storm had passed and the clouds were lifting. They are more hopeful but still hesitant. Assurance and uncertainty intertwined in these to some extent, to paint an encouraged yet somber picture. Finally, "Emerge in the Light" contains those poems that were written when I was feeling especially joyful. The storm had passed, and everything was new. Hope, battered and bruised, had seen me through another crisis, real or imagined.

It is my hope that my poems will inspire you, the reader, to breathe life into that creative spark within you as well.

Acknowledgements

First, I want to acknowledge my sister, Ann, for her support. Ann's reviews and suggestions during this process were invaluable. Thanks, Ann.

Second, three people must be mentioned because they each influenced me in their own unique way when it comes to literature, poems, and writing. All three are retired high school English teachers. Two had been teachers of mine, Charles and Marion Berryhill. The third is my brother-in-law, James Flannigan. Thanks to all!

My good friend Joe also deserves mention. Joe has been with me through many ups and downs, most of which inspired the poems in this collection. Steadfast and true, thanks, Joe, for all you do. Hey, that was sort of a poem in its own right.

Finally, the illustrations in this collection were obtained from thinkstockphotos.com. The exception to this is "Stupid Things," whose illustration was drawn by my daughter, Michelle, and reproduced here with her kind permission.

LOST IN THE DARK

Fool's Lament

Behind the glass you live your life,
Exposed to all who see your strife.
Oblivious to who calls the shots,
Or in whose snare you may be caught.
As all the while, exposed you sit;
As in a corner you pile your shit.
Secure in a farce that seems so real,
For with B. L. you struck the deal.
While across your eyes he pulled the wool.
Covetous, he snatches your family jewels.
Impotent, now without regress;
Hopeless, you're numb to the duress
That darkens the horizon east.
Unaware of the approaching Beast,
You raise your arms in victory's dance,
While demons upon your grave will prance.

Stupid Things

What were you thinking?
What have you done?
You forged on ahead,
Even into the sun.

It melted your wings.
It burned out your eyes.
It blackened your skin.
It ignored all your cries.

Then you forgot
The reason behind
The motive that caused
You forward to grind.

As the sands shifted 'neath
Each measured step,
With feet heavy laden,
Your teary eyes wept.

Too late it came
As you grasped at those rings—
The realization
They were all stupid things.

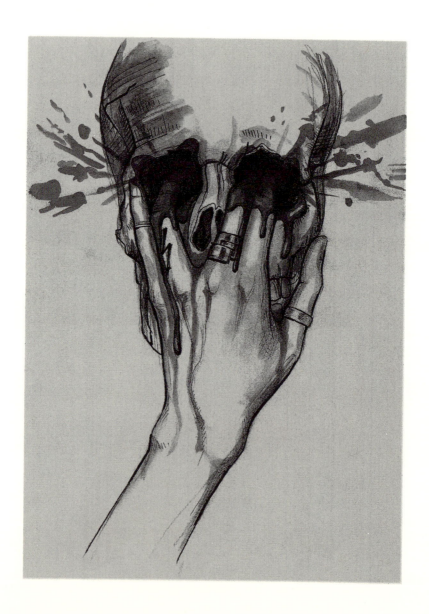

— Hurtful Things —

The angry mind works hard the tongue,
With fiery arrows loosed in rage.
From frustrations ancient as the sun,
Stay in loop; don't turn the page.

Deceitful ways in thought are born,
In afterbirth stained crimson red.
With the remains of innocence gone,
Leaves behind the rotting dead.

So, all these days pass into night,
Darkened by an enraptured heart.
Set free by sloth and glutted pride,
These hurtful things tear one apart.

Pariah

Loser, that's what he is,
As he crawls from hole to hole,
Spreading his disease; a plague-ridden vermin.
Black as night, he has no soul.

Pestilence, avoid his every step.
Turn away as he slithers by.
Close your shutters and bar your doors;
Don't let him in, lest you surely die.

A pariah, curse his putrid name,
His existence to the very last,
As he spirals ever further down,
And in hell's depths his last breath gasp.

Misery

In silence, the night passes
Slowly into day,
Marked only by the beating
Of a wounded heart.
Broken tempo of a thousand drums
Signals a requiem for loves lost
And the passage of another player's part.
Dawn breaks not on this shadowed soul
When the sky stretches in eternal gray,
As he sits alone in misery self-proclaimed,
Awakening to another hopeless day.

Ode to a Worm

Wriggle, my slimy, squirmy friend,
As on my hook you meet your end.
A tiny morsel to catch a fish,
Who then will be a tasty dish.

Irony

Beasts and demons scurry about,
Unseen inside shadows bleak.
I feel their hot breath at my neck,
Tearing at me where I'm weak.
My final ruin seems in little doubt.

Do I cry for heaven's relief,
Hoping angels to my rescue creep,
Or maybe Jesus will avail to me.
The Good Shepherd seeks his lost sheep,
And solidifies my waning belief?

But in the cool, dark night, I walk alone.
No one knocks upon my door.
Deafening silence roars she's near,
A siren's song beckoning toward
A tragic end before His throne.

Lukewarm, neither cold nor hot,
Spewed out to fall upon the ground,
My life in tatters lies in the dust.
Believe! Believe! The resounding sound!
Accept the promise and perish not!

A tattered life can be remade,
While past hurts heal and soon will fade;
But, God, in His eternal love,
Vainly tears what was remade
While I ask forgiveness because *I've* strayed.

Freefall

Come, Lord,
Let her fall!
Night from the heavens,
She envelops me
In her somber light.
While You sigh a knowing breath,
And salvation fades from my sight,
I freefall from a dizzying height.
Lost at once to the sullen day;
Hope's an illusion of Your ethereal way.

Plea

In dark corridors, he wanders through the day.
The embers of a life lived in vain
Cast shadows upon the pockmarked walls.
Spectral opportunities, they slipped away,
Through his fingers greased by foolish dreams
And grasp weakened by naivety's dull refrain.
While those concerned few powerless wait
And watch silently his thrashing gait,
Tethered by chains made link by link,
Forged from a past he can't escape.
"Dear Father," he cries, "hear my plea,
And save me from this tempest sea."

THROUGH THE
TWILIGHT

Three Paths

Three paths through life before us lay,
Though only two are clearly seen.
Unique in course and end each one,
Though difficult they all may seem.

Straight and narrow the first one is.
Direct but difficult remains,
As life's woes buffet every step.
Persevere and riches gain.

The second twists and turns about
Like a drunkard stumbling along.
Without peril, it seems to be.
To Death, this path surely belongs.

The third path, though, is worst of all.
Ne'er straight nor crooked are its ways.
In circles go, to nowhere leads;
The fools and senseless often stray.

The wise man stays his course through life.
Straight paths the sensible endures.
For God desires the truest heart,
While other paths one's death ensures.

Lifted Heart

My heart lifts up.
It soars upon wings renewed
When I dream of you.

Flight

A sweet melody;
Her laugh, on gossamer wings,
Calls his soul to flight.

Aspiration

Things unseen haunt their lonely days
And steal into their empty nights.
Demons tear at sanity's last shred,
Ready to drop them from dizzying heights.

Their eyes meet across troubled existence,
And lock in gaze clouded by uncertain intent.
The comfort of each other's being—
More compelling than two lives unspent.

Two weary souls seeking release
From phantoms that torment their desires.
To be content with what they have,
While reaching for heights to which they aspire.

A Requiem

Waves rush toward the sanded shore
With heaving sighs forevermore;
A woman in climactic throes,
Punctuated by rushing moans.

A hardy few, against the day,
Walk the pier hand in hand
Or huddle in the warming sun,
Oblivious to the pending end.

A cold wind drives the sands below
And sings his mournful, biting song.
While dogged trees hold what remains;
Their hue, reluctantly soon be gone.

As through these eyes I watch it pass,
Quietly, the season falls away.
Succumbing to His steadfast will.
Play *Requiem* for the dying day.

For *K*

Gifted nature,
Yet lost to those dull in brains.
She tells of challenges past
And hopes not yet realized.
Perceived injustice retards her flight,
As she pulls against the binding chains.

Expressive look
Reveals deepest thought,
As hazel eyes flash tone anew.
Sullen mouth imparts tragic woe,
Yet changes to exultant gleam
Of present gladness newly caught.

Childlike manner
Conveys the joy possessed;
It carries her to hope renewed.
In the darkness of a troubled past,
The light of self blazes once more,
Compelling him to hope unaddressed.

This Path Remain

So, the day begins
As he turns the page to the next chapter,
As yet unread.
While the end is known,
The mystery unfolds with each word revealed
While he engaged therein.

As first a vision,
She materialized in ghostly form
Before his eyes,
Worn from sore regret.
Her radiance cast about him in warm embrace,
And thus the act begins.

Sweet laughter gave rise
To renewal of spirits caught up in revelry
As time faded,
Unnoticed while they,
In hopeful courage, succumbed not to the doubt
That tears them from within.

And so he stood at
Life's next journey's start, the One's intention
As yet unknown;
And she, whose purpose
He dares not question but hope against hope will,
For now, this path remain.

Hope Manifested

In the quiet of his mind,
He drifts along on subtle streams
That meander through synaptic forests
And carry him to other dreams.

Memories he recalls come clear:
Deeds past, noble or misguided;
Wrongs and rights committed blindly;
Best of intentions sometimes derided.

Past wounds and hurts in phantom pain
Remind him of the hand-wrought chalice
That cradles a tender-hearted soul
And refines his purpose without malice.

Hope, despite all that he has seen,
A constant companion she has been,
Whispers encouragement through the din
And manifests through you therein.

Sunset

The lake stretches from the bluff;
Opaque glass with texture rough,
Rippled by a painter's brush
Whose hand has lost its steady touch.

To the west, a gap has formed:
A dimpled sky with lake below,
Painted red by the sun's last glow,
Bursting through in his final throw.

The wind now cries his final call.
Cold and sharp, he gives no lull.
The clouds above join as a pall
As the sun sinks quickly, ending all.

We, together, watch the scene
Unfold before us like a dream;
But even now, hope springs anew.
For in that moment, I join with you.

Such Memories

Her blissful face with smile wide,
Translucent hazel laughing eyes,
A greeting offered in tuneful strand,
A warm embrace in lingered stand,
And soft, sweet lips in kiss greet mine.
Such memories sustain my haggard mind.

A joyful laugh that fills the air,
A spirit filled with love and care,
An open mind that seeks to learn.
Kindness's flame within her burns.
Always eager to play her part,
Such memories sustain my somber heart.

These memories of my love sustain
A timeless vision in cerebral grain;
Transcends beyond what I can know,
To foster spirit's ethereal glow;
And within supports a will to cope.
Such memories sustain me in my hope.

Woman

Whose eyes are these that hold my thoughts?
Dark and warm, their sultry gaze
Sifts through the contents of my soul and, like fire,
Burns deeply into my conscious haze.

Whose smile is this that melts my heart?
It warms the essence of my day,
Restoring purpose to my being and, like flame,
Lights the path as I go my way.

Whose voice is this that soothes my ear?
The sweetest sound, it ever rings.
Strings and harp pale in beauty, and, by God ordained,
Angels fall silent when she sings.

What woman is this whose hand I hold?
With gentleness, she treats my soul.
She cares for wounds I cannot hide and, with practiced hands,
Heals my being to make me whole.

My Love

In darkness, she's a beacon light.
When blinded, she gives me welcomed sight.
Wounded, she takes away the pain.
Storm tossed, she stops the driving rain.
Her smile shames the brightest moon.
Her laugh can make the songbirds swoon.
When sad, she offers relieving cheer.
When troubled, she takes the darkest fear.
Her presence calms the tempest sea.
My love throughout remains with me.

Starry Night

Oh, starry night
With tiny drops of silver hue
On velvet canvas, darkest black,
Rimmed by soft glow of city light.

A ghostly ship
Hangs above in delicate frame
And dissipates before my eyes,
While a train blows its lonely refrain.

A soft voice
Whispers secrets in my ear
And echoes her playful laugh,
While the cool night lingers near.

Dawn

The sun breaks over a tree-topped ridge,
Bathing the field below in cool shades of gray,
While a light mist hangs on chilled morning air
And birds sing their symphony to greet the day.

Nimble clouds dot the morning sky,
Embraced by the sun's warm, caressing light.
They hang suspended in shifting blues,
While hues pink and red paint the horizon bright.

Such beauty, so wondrous to behold,
Inspires my heart and spirit renews.
For heaven's glory in this scene displayed,
The eternal hand creates each day anew.

In this way, my love restores my soul
And to my person brings such kindness
That clears the cobwebs from my mind
And from sad eyes removes the blindness.

Her presence, like a blanket warm,
When troubled by uncertain plight,
As coming dawn brings new day's hope,
She whispers softly, "It will be all right."

Trees

The green and rust stand together.
Soon one will fall like a feather,
To be reborn in spring's cool dawn,
While the other holds its color on.

Revelation's Light

What light have I to guide my steps?
Stumbling through the murky haze,
I thrash about to find my way,
As time unfolds to endless days.

The path through forest deep winds on,
Where eerie darkness hides the end,
And footsteps echo in the void,
Drawn to the depths of hell descend.

The lie supplants substantive things.
Oblivious now to all that's real,
Trust gives way to ethereal evil,
As demons work the final seal.

But hope eternal, even now,
Drives away the deepest fears,
And God, in His splendor pure,
Wipes away the saddest tears.

The darkest shadows disappear,
Driven from recesses deep.
The Word in flesh, revelation's light,
From fallen world calls in His sheep.

Refuge

Even in her warm embrace,
Darkness now o'ertakes my soul
And envelops me in his cold grasp.
His breath surrounds me in a sickly rasp.

Tossed about in tempest seas,
Rigging torn and fallen masts,
The storm builds now, violent within.
My heart is vanquished by the raging din.

I hold on to tenuous dream.
Cruel night, starless in repose,
She taunts me with her beckoning rasp
And leaves me wayward as the die is cast.

Where are You, oh Lord, my God?
Hopeless, I am tossed about.
My pleas echo in the widening void,
Left bewildered, surely to be destroyed.

Yet, God is with me even here.
His power I see in gale winds.
His voice I hear in the ocean's roar.
His love is evident through life restored.

In Your bosom refuge waits.
Though demons lurk at my door
And Satan boldly sings his dirges,
In Your embrace, my confidence emerges.

Greater Things

Pink highlights a dappled field blue.
Brilliant red, the sun breaks through,
Exploding above the horizon's dark'ning hue,
As passing day gives way to nighttime new.

Now, the dusk in silence passes,
While angels call their somber masses.
As the setting sun his final gasp does take,
Wild things from their deepest slumber wake.

In silence, the road slips ever onward.
The sky in darkness lingers upward.
Alone, in dream, I spiral forward
And wonder if I'm sliding backward.

In that moment, He seems real
And breaks the melancholy that I feel.
His still, small voice whispers now to me,
"Hold on, my child; greater things you'll see."

EMERGE IN
THE LIGHT

Reborn

The wind across the water blows,
While ripples form in chiseled rows
That grow and undulate in time
And lose all reason and all rhyme.

With raging cries and foam-topped crest,
In force they march from out the west
And crash upon the steadfast shore,
To make their mark forever more.

The sands give in to shaping tide,
As waves upon the beach do ride.
The shoreline alters through the days,
As currents move in practiced ways.

The bluffs that rise majestic'ly
Above the lake with enmity,
Eventually must retreat
With breakers surging at their feet.

On this, my thoughts are captive bound,
A picture of God's glory crowned.
The forces that reshape the land
In life are like the Master's hand.

His spirit moves to sculpt my hope
Of living waters, eager tope.
For Christ, in splendor now adorned
While through His blood I am reborn.

The Light (My Child)

Enter into the light, my child.
Bathe in His redemptive grace.
The darkness fades into the past,
As with each step increase your pace.

Enter into the light, my child.
Urgent now, hasten your stride.
Emerge from lonely, sinful night.
Arise anew as the old self dies.

Enter into the light, my child.
Yesterday's tears now forgotten.
Old deeds, like dead skin, slough away,
Burned up in the presence of the Son.

Enter into the light, my child.
Fear in this place has no hold.
Boldly proclaim a life renewed,
As evil retreats into the void.

Stand in the light, my child!
Fear not death or demon's sting.
Reflect His glory that gives you hope,
And share the light that salvation brings.

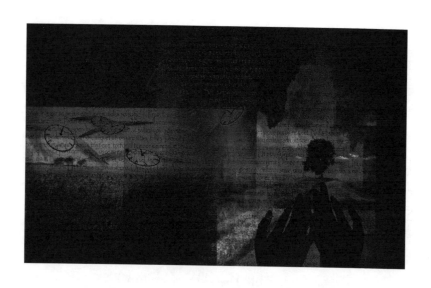

From Darkness (Rise New)

Darkness envelops a haggard soul drawn.
Chains, forged in avenues traveled well nigh,
Hold a life captive in prison cell bare,
Trapped inside walls wrought from schemes gone awry.

Hopeless—each day bleeds, then, into one dream.
Starless night stretches in blackened descent.
Into the night, urgent pleas go forth hence.
Mercy now sought for the wrongs from time spent.

Blackness recedes; the void's made full once more.
Out of His grace, life is wrought from ash bleak;
Glory's salvation from God's purpose true.
Christ, in love, beckons, "From darkness, rise new."

Thankful Praise

The Word spoke into the darkness,
Casting light into endless void;
Creation graced eternity,
As witness to God's trinity.

Life, with the spoken word released,
Sprang from emptiness at God's call;
Proof of His majesty now told;
Splendors too wond'rous to behold.

Who can fathom Your mind, oh God,
Or comprehend Your love's fullness,
Or criticize the works You've wrought,
Or doubt our freedom that You bought?

Powerful is Your hand, oh God,
And endless Your creative ways.
With thankful praise, we call Your name
And rejoice for when our Savior came.

Hope's Delight

The universe explodes in time,
Blinding white in majestic silence,
Scattering stars into the void,
Created new in sparkling brilliance.

Tender shoots push through the earth,
As seeds open in hopeful promise.
They reach skyward toward the sun,
To bless us through His plan flawless.

Now each day the sun rises new,
Nurturing the world arrayed below;
Awakening life to promise renewed.
In sacrifice, its purpose bestows.

As deep, dark eyes look into his,
They sparkle as the starry night.
Soft visage breaks in gracious smile
And testify to new hope's delight.

Full Moon

Bathing Earth below,
Like mother caressing child,
She is ever near.

Mother/Daughter

Radiant faces smile in unison,
Twin moons in a starless night,
While piercing eyes laugh as one,
And beaming smiles express delight.
Mother hovers above in love,
As daughter expresses hopeful light.

Manifested

Shrouded in a muddled night,
The moon glows an ethereal light
That casts pale upon creation
And echoes of the world's foundation.

While the sky breathes a heavy sigh,
As it settles in for twilight nigh,
The breeze whispers a soft refrain
Of another day's spent remains.

Stand I, alone, bathed in this scene,
Joyful in the moment serene,
Reminded of His eternal love,
Manifested through You thereof.

Smile

Beaming bright and warm,
As the sun at apogee,
Her smile warms my heart.

Radiance

Radiant as an angel's face.
Glowing with the warmest trace.
Bluest eyes that sparkle bright.
A smile that radiates with light.
Framed by locks of auburn hair.
With this vision, few can compare.

Breathe

Oh love, a frail tapestry,
Now offer it I do to thee.
Please take my hand in revelry,
And hold my heart so carefully.
So, wake my soul from dormancy,
To bring my spirit ecstasy.
I wait for you so patiently.
My purpose cries relentlessly,
For you are all my eyes can see;
As I pursue you zealously,
For in my life new life you breathe.

Endnote

1   The idea of an "origin" I discovered while reading Dietrich Bonhoeffer's *Ethics*. Dietrich Bonhoeffer (1906 – 1945) was a Lutheran minister who used his position to resist Adolf Hitler and the Nazi regime in Germany. He was hanged by the Nazi's shortly before Germany's surrender. Bonhoeffer used "origin" in his writing to refer to the Christian God. To learn more, please refer to:

Bonhoeffer, Dietrich (1995). *Ethics*. New York: Touchstone.

About the Author

A. E. Fonner grew up in southwestern Pennsylvania. After spending six years in the US Navy, he settled in Illinois but moved on to other opportunities after ten years. The father of two adult daughters, he currently lives in southwestern Michigan and works in quality assurance in the electrical generating industry. He holds a bachelor of science degree in technical management from DeVry University and has self-published one novel, Ones Such as These.